SPOTLIGHTS

PREHISTORIC LIFE

Written by Dougal Dixon

SIMON & SCHUSTER
YOUNG BOOKS

ACKNOWLEDGMENTS

Illustrated by
Joanne Cowne
Brin Edwards
Denys Ovenden
Elizabeth Sawyer
Andrew Tewson

Picture credits
Front cover SPL / Jim Amos

First published in 1993 by
Simon & Schuster Young Books
Simon & Schuster Limited
Campus 400
Maylands Avenue
Hemel Hempstead
Herts HP2 7EZ

Planned and produced by
Andromeda Oxford Limited
11-15 The Vineyard
Abingdon
Oxon OX14 3PX

Copyright © Andromeda Oxford Limited 1993
Reprinted 1993

ISBN 0-7500-1417-2
Printed in Singapore by Kim Hup Lee

CONTENTS

INTRODUCTION

This book looks at the Earth before people became the dominant creature on the planet. Our planet is many thousands of millions of years old and has seen many strange and wonderful animals and plants come and go – at first life was only found in the sea but later the land was also colonised. Eventually continents were ruled by communities of creatures that have long since disappeared. How do we know about all these things? Scientists are able to discover many facts about these lost worlds from studying rocks and the remains (fossils) of long-dead creatures that have been preserved in them.

FINDING FOSSILS

Some fossils are quite common. Many of the items in this book should be quite easy to find if you are in the right area, where the rocks date from the right period. These include ammonites, trilobites and other sea-living invertebrates. Others, however, such as dinosaur skeletons, are very rare finds, indeed. You are going to have to look for them in museums.

HOW TO USE THIS BOOK

This book explores and explains the world of prehistoric life. The book begins with the oldest types of animals and plants and takes the reader through the creatures of the main geological periods up to the Ice Ages.

INTRODUCTION

Concise yet highly informative, this text introduces the reader to the animals and plants shown. This broad coverage is complemented by more detailed exploration of particular points in the numerous captions.

HEADING

The subject matter of each spread is clearly identified by a heading prominently displayed in the top left-hand corner.

ILLUSTRATIONS

High quality, full colour artwork bring the world of prehistoric animals and plants to life. Each spread is packed with visual information.

SPOTLIGHTS

A series of illustrations at the bottom of each page encourages the reader to look out for easy to find or important fossils that can be found in museums.

TWO-FOOTED

Although most plant-eating dinosaurs walked about on fours, there was a large group could walk on two feet. The a hip-bone with a gap bene the big plant-digesting gut c be carried between the legs a animal could still balance.
These upright dinosaurs, su Iguanodon, evolved in the late Triassic period but they really came into their own in Cretace times. The later types had very strong grinding teeth and cheek pouches, so that they could eat tough conifer needles.

SPRINTERS
Lightweight plant-eaters, like the 2m-long *Hypsilophodon*, were built for speed and could run fast to escape danger.

LOOK OUT FOR THESE

EDMONTOSAURUS
The skeleton of the duckbill *Edmonto-saurus* shows the gap beneath the hips. The long tail would have helped it to balance.

DETAILED INFORMATION

From the latest theories on the lifestyles of dinosaurs to the formation of the coal forests, the reader is given a wealth of information to help appreciate the prehistoric world.

GEOLOGICAL TIME

The history of the Earth covers vast spans of time – hundreds of millions of years. To make sense of such huge figures, geologists divide time up into geological 'periods' and 'eras'. Just as in human history we talk about Pre-Columbian America, Victorian Britain, Tang Dynasty China – associating time with the events that happened then – so geologists divide time into the Age of Fishes, the Age of Reptiles, the Age of Mammals, and so on, based on the types of animals that evolved then.

These different periods are given names, and rocks that were laid down during each period can be identified by the types of fossils they contain. Usually geological time is shown as a column, with the oldest periods and eras at the bottom, and the more recent at the top.

INSET ARTWORKS

Animals or aspects of behaviour that help to explain particular points are shown in inset, along with an explanation of their significance.

REFERENCE TAB

These colour tabs are keyed into the geological time-scale (shown right) so that the period shown can be found quickly and easily.

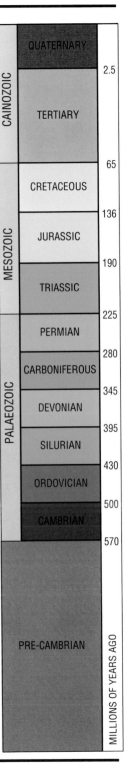

Era	Period	Millions of years ago
CAINOZOIC	QUATERNARY	
		2.5
	TERTIARY	
		65
MESOZOIC	CRETACEOUS	
		136
	JURASSIC	
		190
	TRIASSIC	
		225
PALAEOZOIC	PERMIAN	
		280
	CARBONIFEROUS	
		345
	DEVONIAN	
		395
	SILURIAN	
		430
	ORDOVICIAN	
		500
	CAMBRIAN	
		570
	PRE-CAMBRIAN	

MILLIONS OF YEARS AGO

ERS

WO.

RS
oted
s, like the

THUMB SPIKE
The hand was shaped like a boxing glove with a spike for a thumb which they used in fights.

lived in
may
ome of
all
sed
e snout
es.

DUCKBILLS
The most important group of plant-eaters in the late Cretaceous period were the duck-billed dinosaurs, such as *Edmontosaurus*. Some had strange crests on their heads.

PARASAUROLOPHUS
The longest crest of all was found on this duckbill. It was a hollow tube linked to e nose.

CORYTHOSAURUS
This was a large duckbill with a hollow crest like an ancient Greek hat.

SAUROLOPHUS
Some duckbill crests were solid spikes. It is now thought that different sexes had different-sized crests.

NESTS
Dinosaurs laid eggs in nests. This is known because fossil nesting sites belong...

SECRETS IN STONE

How do we find out about life on Earth long, long ago?

The secret lies in the fossils. These are the remains of the animals and plants that existed in past times, and have become preserved in the rocks. Only a tiny fraction of the Earth's living things have become fossils. Even if their remains are buried before they rot, the sediment in which they are buried may be disturbed later and the remains destroyed. Then, if they do become fossils, Earth movements may destroy the surrounding rocks and the fossils with them. For us to discover them they must become exposed at the surface. A typical fossilization sequence is shown on the right.

ANIMAL DIES
Usually when an animal dies its body is quickly eaten up by scavengers, or it rots away. The body has to be preserved quickly or it will be lost.

BURIED UNDER SAND
If the animal falls into a river its body may be covered up by sand before it decays.

LOOK OUT FOR THESE

■ **INSECT IN AMBER**
An insect may be trapped in resin which seeps from a tree. It will then be preserved when the resin is buried and turns to amber.

■ **ORIGINAL BONES**
The hard parts of an animal may be preserved, like this bone of a mammal from the Ice Age tar pits in Los Angeles.

■ **CARBONIZATION**
A fossil plant may consist of a thin film of the carbon which the plant originally contained. Masses of these fossils crammed together make coal.

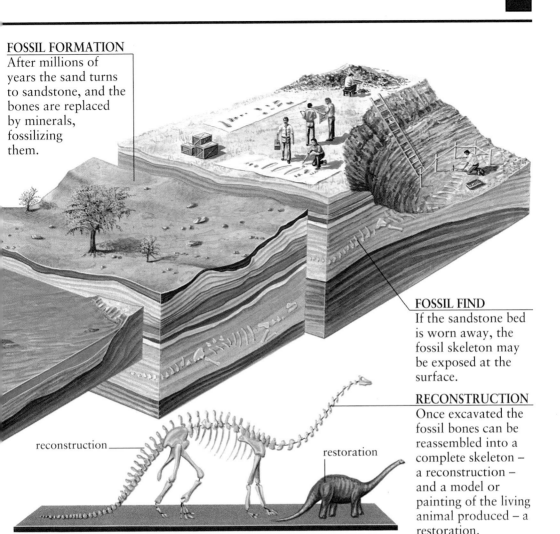

FOSSIL FORMATION

After millions of years the sand turns to sandstone, and the bones are replaced by minerals, fossilizing them.

FOSSIL FIND

If the sandstone bed is worn away, the fossil skeleton may be exposed at the surface.

RECONSTRUCTION

Once excavated the fossil bones can be reassembled into a complete skeleton – a reconstruction – and a model or painting of the living animal produced – a restoration.

reconstruction

restoration

PETRIFIED WOOD

In some fossils, the original material has been replaced by minerals from the rocks. You can still see the original structure.

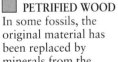

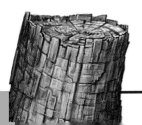

MOULD

The dead material may rot away after being buried, leaving a hole in the rock. This is called a mould fossil.

CAST

If a mould fills up with minerals (deposited from water seeping through the rock), it becomes a cast fossil.

TRACE FOSSIL

Fossil footprints or worm tracks, showing where an animal has been, are called trace fossils.

THE EARLIEST FOSSILS

The earliest good fossils date from 570 million years ago – the beginning of the Cambrian period in the Earth's history. Before then, animals had no hard parts and so did not fossilize well.

As soon as hard shells evolved, all kinds of different animals appeared. It was as if nature were trying out different shapes and designs to see what would work. Most of these early creatures died out after a few million years, but the rest went on to evolve into the later animals.

Cambrian fossils are found all over the world, but many thousands of different types have been collected at one place in the Rocky Mountains in Canada. These are the Burgess Shale fossils which give us a good idea of what life was like on the Cambrian sea floor.

JOINTED ANIMALS
Many early animals, such as *Marella*, had skeletons with joints, like insects.

HUNTERS
Opabinia was a fierce little animal that hunted for food along the seabed.

LOOK OUT FOR THESE

MARELLA
Bristly, swimming animal with a shield-like head, about 2cm long.

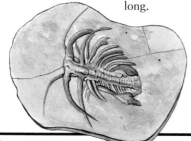

OPABINIA
With jaws on the end of a trunk, and five eyes, it was like nothing that lives today.

AMISKWIA
The conditions for preservation in the Burgess Shale were so good that even soft-bodied animals left good fossils.

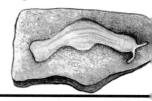

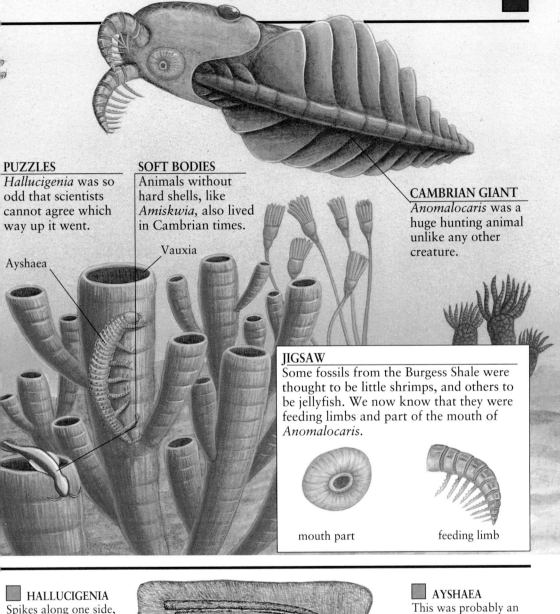

PUZZLES
Hallucigenia was so odd that scientists cannot agree which way up it went.

SOFT BODIES
Animals without hard shells, like *Amiskwia*, also lived in Cambrian times.

CAMBRIAN GIANT
Anomalocaris was a huge hunting animal unlike any other creature.

Vauxia

Ayshaea

JIGSAW
Some fossils from the Burgess Shale were thought to be little shrimps, and others to be jellyfish. We now know that they were feeding limbs and part of the mouth of *Anomalocaris*.

mouth part

feeding limb

■ HALLUCIGENIA
Spikes along one side, tentacles along the other, a bulb at one end and a trunk at the other – no wonder no-one is sure what it did or how it lived!

■ VAUXIA
A large sponge that lived in colonies on the Cambrian seabed.

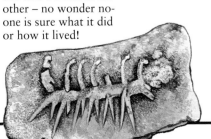

■ AYSHAEA
This was probably an ancestor of a group of animals called the velvet worms. It fed on sponges.

THE SILURIAN REEF

In the Silurian period, most creatures still lived in the sea, and the fossils from that time are nearly all of marine animals. Near the shores of the continents, the waters were warm and shallow. There, great reefs, made up mainly of sponges, were able to grow. Trilobites were common, and so were starfish and their relatives the sea-lilies. Most of the shellfish were from a group called the brachiopods. The reefs produced masses of limy sediments. These have become fossil-rich limestones.

REEF-BUILDERS
Silurian reefs were built from the skeletons of sponges, like this *Ischadites*.

CORALS
Most Silurian corals were solitary types, like sea-anemones in limy cups.

ANCIENT SNAILS
Some snails, like this *Platyceras,* lived among the forests of sea-lilies.

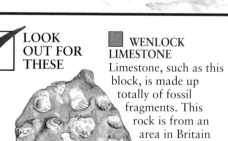

LOOK OUT FOR THESE

WENLOCK LIMESTONE
Limestone, such as this block, is made up totally of fossil fragments. This rock is from an area in Britain where the seas were clear enough for large reefs to form.

ISCHADITES
Reef-building sponges can be branching or rounded, like this fossil of *Ischadites*.

GISSOCRINUS
Sea-lilies may be found complete with their stalks, like this specimen of *Gissocrinus*, or just as a collection of broken pieces.

STALKED STARFISH
Sea-lilies or crinoids, like these *Gissocrinus*, were like upside-down starfish on long stalks.

BRACHIOPODS
Brachiopods looked like modern bivalve shellfish because they evolved the same lifestyle.

COMPOUND CORALS
Some corals were made up of many animals packed closely together, like modern types.

TOP AND BOTTOM
Bivalves have a left shell and a right shell. Brachiopods, like *Meristina*, have a top shell and a bottom shell.

FAVOSITES
In a compound coral, like *Favosites*, each hole held an individual coral animal separated from its neighbour by a thin wall.

MERISTINA
Meristina was a brachiopod with a smooth shell that lived on the seabed during the Silurian period.

PLATYCERAS
Gastropods – the snails – are among the oldest fossils. This one has a hooked tip to the shell.

TRILOBITES

The arthropods are a major group of animals that developed in the Cambrian period. They have jointed bodies and jointed legs. One type, called the trilobites, dominated the seas in Cambrian, Ordovician and Silurian times, and even hung on until the Permian before becoming extinct.

They looked a little like modern woodlice, or sow-bugs, but lived in the sea. The many different kinds had a wide range of lifestyles, but they all had a shell that was divided into a headshield, a jointed back and a tailshield. They had many pairs of legs and gills underneath.

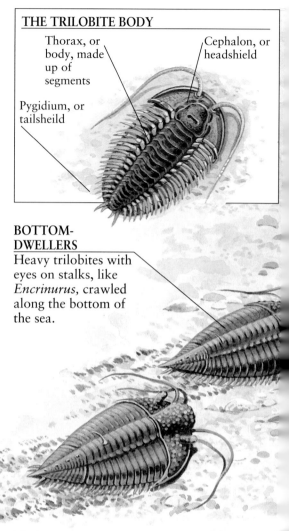

THE TRILOBITE BODY

Thorax, or body, made up of segments

Cephalon, or headshield

Pygidium, or tailsheild

BOTTOM-DWELLERS
Heavy trilobites with eyes on stalks, like *Encrinurus*, crawled along the bottom of the sea.

 **LOOK OUT FOR THESE**

■ **PRIMITIVE TYPE**
The earliest trilobites, like *Paradoxides*, had no tailshield.

■ **ROLLED-UP FOSSIL**
Trilobites sometimes died while rolled up, such as in this fossil.

■ **COMPLETE TRILOBITE**
It is very rare to find one with legs and antennae. This one is *Olenoides*.

■ **MASS GRAVE**
Trilobites were so common that sometimes many of them were fossilized together in the same piece of rock.

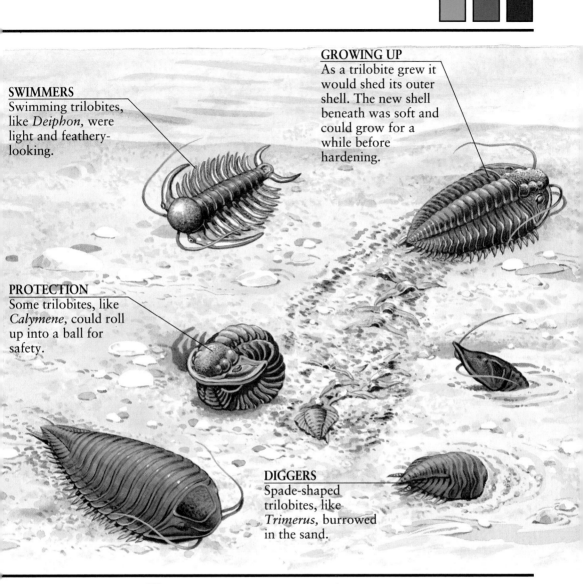

SWIMMERS
Swimming trilobites, like *Deiphon*, were light and feathery-looking.

GROWING UP
As a trilobite grew it would shed its outer shell. The new shell beneath was soft and could grow for a while before hardening.

PROTECTION
Some trilobites, like *Calymene*, could roll up into a ball for safety.

DIGGERS
Spade-shaped trilobites, like *Trimerus*, burrowed in the sand.

PYGIDIUM
Shell pieces, such as the tailshield (pygidium), were shed many times during the trilobite's life, so one trilobite could produce many fossils.

CEPHALON
Parts of the shell, such as the headshield (cephalon), are more common as fossils than the whole animal.

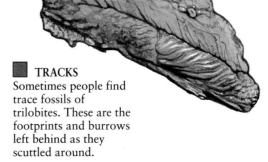

TRACKS
Sometimes people find trace fossils of trilobites. These are the footprints and burrows left behind as they scuttled around.

15

FISH

During the Ordovician and Silurian periods, fish were beginning to evolve. By the Devonian, they were well established in the sea and were spreading into rivers and lakes.

The earliest fish had no jaws – just suckers. Later, jaws and armour developed. Some fish had skeletons of bone. Others had skeletons of horny gristle. Many even developed lungs and muscular fins and could spend some time out of the water. These were the ancestors of all the animals with backbones (vertebrates) which lived on the land.

SPINY SHARKS
The 'spiny sharks', like *Climatius*, had rows of tiny fins along the belly.

FIERCE JAWS
Fish with complex jaws, scales and plates, such as *Coccosteus*, soon evolved.

ARMOUR
Bothriolepis was an early form of fish. The head and front half were protected by armoured plates.

LOOK OUT FOR THESE

FISH HEADSHIELD
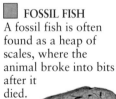
The headshield of this jawless fish looks rather like the headshield of a trilobite.

FOSSIL FISH
A fossil fish is often found as a heap of scales, where the animal broke into bits after it died.

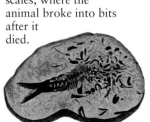

FISH BED
When a lake dried up, the fish gathered in the last puddle and died. They are all found fossilized together, like these *Holoptychius*.

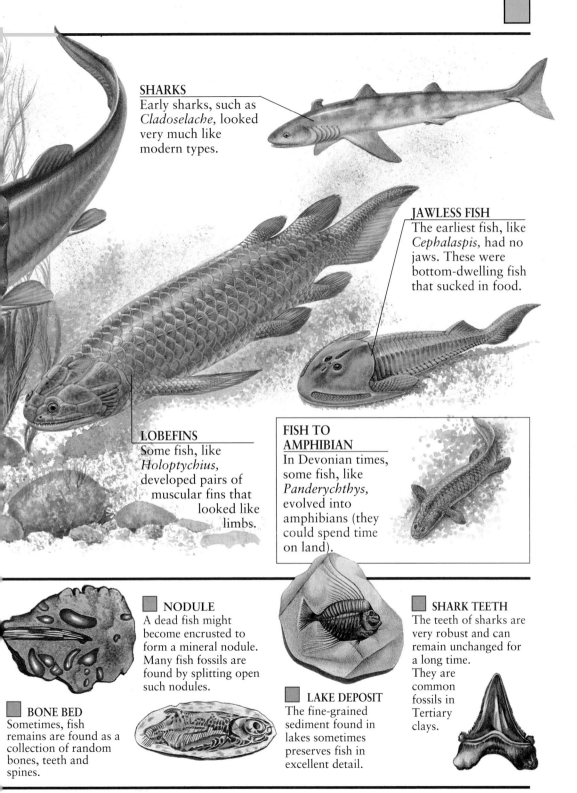

SHARKS
Early sharks, such as *Cladoselache*, looked very much like modern types.

JAWLESS FISH
The earliest fish, like *Cephalaspis*, had no jaws. These were bottom-dwelling fish that sucked in food.

LOBEFINS
Some fish, like *Holoptychius*, developed pairs of muscular fins that looked like limbs.

FISH TO AMPHIBIAN
In Devonian times, some fish, like *Panderychthys*, evolved into amphibians (they could spend time on land).

NODULE
A dead fish might become encrusted to form a mineral nodule. Many fish fossils are found by splitting open such nodules.

BONE BED
Sometimes, fish remains are found as a collection of random bones, teeth and spines.

LAKE DEPOSIT
The fine-grained sediment found in lakes sometimes preserves fish in excellent detail.

SHARK TEETH
The teeth of sharks are very robust and can remain unchanged for a long time. They are common fossils in Tertiary clays.

THE COAL FORESTS

Imagine a world in which primitive plants grew as tall as trees, and dragonflies as large as birds flew through the air. In fact, this environment was once widespread in Europe, Asia and North America. These were the great Carboniferous coal forests that first appeared 350 million years ago and lasted for nearly 70 million years. The remains of these plants became seams of coal.

The forests grew in shallow coastal estuaries. As water levels rose, large areas of forest died.

HORSETAILS
Giant horsetails had hollow trunks, and whorls of leaves on the stem.

DRAGONFLIES
Large dragonflies bred in shallow waters. Some had wings over 30cm wide.

ROTTING PLANTS
As the plants rotted they turned into a substance called peat. The lowest layers slowly turned to coal.

LOOK OUT FOR THESE

LEPIDODENDRON
A 30m tall scale tree, it was common in coal forests of Europe and North America during the Carboniferous. Smaller relatives – the clubmosses – survive today.

CALAMITES
Widespread in coal forests during the Carboniferous. Whorls of up to 50 leaves on trunk. Only smaller horsetails survive.

ANNULARIA
A relative of the living horsetails, the most commonly found remains are fossil leaves.

BRANCHES
Many of these simple plants had branches which were divided into two equal parts.

FOSSIL LEAVES
The leaves of these great trees can often be found in coal.

AMPHIBIANS
The shallow pools and rivers were full of fish and early forms of amphibians.

ROOTS
The branched root systems of the trees gave strong support in soils and water.

STIGMARIA
Fossil fragments of underground branches, bearing scars or 'stigmata' on the surface.

NEUROPTERIS
Up to 5m tall. Seed bearing fern of the Carboniferous. Similar in size and appearance to tree ferns today.

ALETHOPTERIS
Fern with fronds up to 1m. Common in Upper Carboniferous. Similar in appearance to modern day bracken.

EARLY REPTILES AND AMPHIBIANS

Gradually, the great swampy coal forests of the Carboniferous period died away, and were replaced by vast areas of desert in Permian times. The numbers of amphibians, which needed watery conditions in which to lay their eggs, dwindled. Some became big, dry land animals, but for the most part, the reptiles took over. Reptile eggs were encased in a waterproof shell and could be laid on land.

PLANT-EATERS
Some early reptiles became plant-eaters, like *Edaphosaurus*. Their temperature regulation system, using their great fins, later developed into a mammal's warm-bloodedness.

REPTILE EVOLUTION
Two main reptile groups evolved in the Permian and Triassic periods. The first were the mammal-like reptiles. The second main group were the thecodonts. They began as crocodile-like animals. These reptiles were to develop into the dinosaurs.

Mammal-like reptiles

Cynognathus

Dimetrodon

Thecodonts

Euparkeria

Araeoscelis

FIN BACKS
Dimetrodon also had a large fin on its back. The large surface of the fin enabled it to warm up and cool down quickly.

LOOK OUT FOR THESE

WESTLOTHIANA
This was the earliest known reptile. It was like a little lizard. The only fossil was found in early Carboniferous rocks in Scotland.

DIMETRODON
The fossil of *Dimetrodon* shows long spines sticking up from the backbone. These must have supported a sail.

FOOTPRINTS
Some animals are known only from footprints left in the Permian desert sand. *Cheirotherium* is the name given to these.

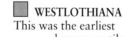

RULING REPTILES
At the beginning of the Permian period, the reptiles that were to develop into the dinosaurs were small and lizard-like, such as *Araeoscelis*.

LAND AMPHIBIANS
Heavy land-living amphibians like *Eryops*, which had strong legs and jaws, lived at the desert edges.

WATER AMPHIBIANS
Water-based amphibians, like *Diplocaulus* with its odd-shaped head, still lived in oases.

THECODONT
Early thecodonts lived in the water. Later, land-living types had long hind legs and a long tail, originally for swimming.

ERYOPS
In Permian times some of the big amphibians, such as *Eryops,* had enormous heads, sometimes more than 1m long.

CYNOGNATHUS
The skull of this mammal-like reptile shows killing teeth and nipping teeth, just like a mammal.

SEA REPTILES

The reptiles not only dominated the land, but some even returned to live in the sea. In the Triassic and Jurassic periods, two important groups of marine reptiles, the plesiosaurs and the ichthyosaurs, evolved. These reptiles were well adapted to a seagoing life with their streamlined shape and paddle-like limbs. They existed mainly on a diet of fish and ammonites (see page 26) but often fed on one another.

MOSASAURS

In the Cretaceous period, the ichthyosaurs died out, but their place was taken by huge sea lizards called mosasaurs, such as *Platycarpus*. All the marine reptiles had died out by the end of the Cretaceous period.

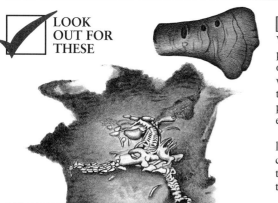

LONG NECKS

Elasmosaurs, such as *Cryptoclidus*, were long-necked plesiosaurs.

LOOK OUT FOR THESE

PLESIOSAUR

We know that plesiosaurs attacked one another because we have found toothmarks from pliosaurs cut deep into elasmosaur bones.

Skeletons of sea-living animals are more common, because things fossilize easily at the bottom of the sea.

ICHTHYOSAUR BACKBONES

The disc-shaped backbones (vertebrae) of ichthyosaurs are often found in rocks from Jurassic times.

FISH-LIKE REPTILES
Ichthyosaurs were
the most fish-like
reptiles.
Ichthyosaurus
looked rather like a
shark or even a
dolphin.

SHORT NECKS
Pliosaurs, such as
Peloneustes, were
short-necked, big-
headed, whale-like
plesiosaurs.

**BABY
ICHTHYOSAUR**
Ichthyosaurs from a
site in Germany still
show their soft tissues.
Some are even giving
birth.

**ICHTHYOSAUR
JAWS**
Ichthyosaurs had
many sharp teeth. This
feature shows they
caught slippery things
like fish and
ammonites.

MOSASAURUS
The first fossil of a
giant reptile ever to be
discovered was the
jawbone of
Mosasaurus, in the
Netherlands in 1770.

TOOTHMARKS
Fossils of ammonite
shells with mosasaur
toothmarks show that
mosasaurs ate these
animals.

FLYING REPTILES

At the time the marine reptiles and the ammonites dominated the seas, and the dinosaurs stalked the land, the skies were ruled by another group of reptiles – the pterosaurs.

SHORT-TAILED PTEROSAURS
More advanced pterosaurs, like *Pterodactylus* and *Anurognathus* had short tails and long wrists.

TYPICAL PTEROSAUR
Peteinosaurus had a furry lightweight body and leathery wings attached to immensely long fourth fingers.

LONG-TAILED PTEROSAURS
Primitive pterosaurs, like *Rhamphorhynchus*, had long tails and short wrists.

LOOK OUT FOR THESE

COMPLETE SKELETON
A complete pterosaur skeleton, like this *Pterodactylus*, often has the head thrown back. This shows how the body dried out before it was buried.

FUR
The small pterosaur *Sordes* has been preserved complete with its body fur.

THE WINGFINGER
The bones of the fourth finger, which supported the wing, were as thick as those of the arm.

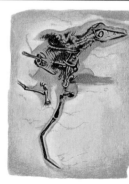

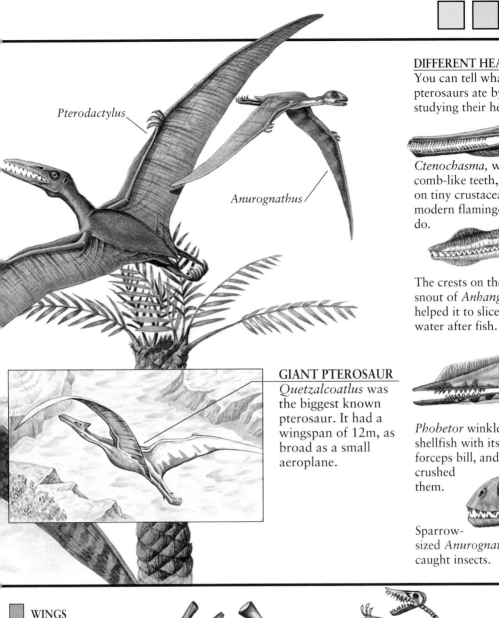

Pterodactylus

Anurognathus

GIANT PTEROSAUR

Quetzalcoatlus was the biggest known pterosaur. It had a wingspan of 12m, as broad as a small aeroplane.

DIFFERENT HEADS

You can tell what pterosaurs ate by studying their heads.

Ctenochasma, with its comb-like teeth, fed on tiny crustaceans, as modern flamingoes do.

The crests on the snout of *Anhanguera* helped it to slice the water after fish.

Phobetor winkled out shellfish with its forceps bill, and crushed them.

Sparrow-sized *Anurognathus* caught insects.

WINGS

The sediments of Solnhofen in Germany are very fine, so they often preserve the imprint of the wing.

BONES

People sometimes find individual pieces of broken pterosaur bone while fossil-hunting in Jurassic and Cretaceous rocks.

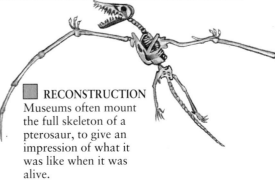

RECONSTRUCTION

Museums often mount the full skeleton of a pterosaur, to give an impression of what it was like when it was alive.

THE TEEMING SEAS

The seas from the Triassic to the Cretaceous teemed with life, and fossils of all kinds of creatures were left. The most famous are probably the ammonites.

Ammonites were relatives of the octopus and squid, but they lived in coiled shells. The shells had interesting patterns and shapes. Ammonites were common and evolved quickly. This makes them very useful to geologists who can tell how old a bed of rock is by identifying the type of ammonite fossils in it.

SWIMMERS
An ammonite with a narrow disc-like shell, like *Mantelliceras*, was probably a swimmer and a hunter.

CUTAWAY
An ammonite shell was divided into chambers. The wall of each chamber met the outside wall in a wiggly line called the suture line. The shape of this line is useful in identifying an ammonite. The living animal occupied the last whorl of the shell.

 **LOOK OUT FOR THESE**

SUTURE LINES
Often, the shell of an ammonite has worn away, and the suture lines are visible.

SHELL SHAPES
Some ammonite shells have ribs. Some have a distinct keel. Some, like *Harpoceras*, have both.

SHELL PATTERNS
An ammonite shell may be decorated with tubercles, like *Schloenbachia*.

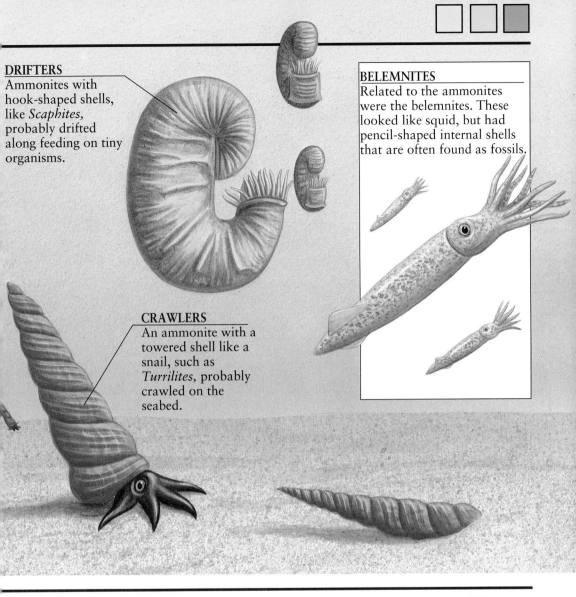

DRIFTERS
Ammonites with hook-shaped shells, like *Scaphites*, probably drifted along feeding on tiny organisms.

BELEMNITES
Related to the ammonites were the belemnites. These looked like squid, but had pencil-shaped internal shells that are often found as fossils.

CRAWLERS
An ammonite with a towered shell like a snail, such as *Turrilites*, probably crawled on the seabed.

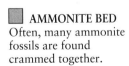

AMMONITE BED
Often, many ammonite fossils are found crammed together.

BELEMNITE HOOKS
Fossil belemnite shells are common. But it is rare to find traces of the tiny hooks they carried on their tentacles.

OCTOPUS
The earliest octopus fossil was found in Jurassic rocks. It is unusual for an octopus – an animal without a shell or skeleton – to be fossilized.

SHELL SECTION
Ammonites are often split across and polished. Minerals filling the chambers produce a pattern.

HUNTING DINOSAURS

Of all the animals that ever walked the Earth, probably the dinosaurs were the most spectacular. Some dinosaurs were fast running, small creatures, others were lumbering giants. But the great meat-eaters were the most awe-inspiring.

The meat-eating dinosaurs were the first to evolve, in the Triassic period.

The early types fed on other reptiles, insects and probably the first mammals as well. Later forms of dinosaurs were enormous and fed on other dinosaurs. Many different types lived at the same time, each specializing in a different kind of hunting.

AMBUSHERS
Some dinosaurs, like *Allosaurus*, were big enough to hunt and kill the biggest plant-eating dinosaurs.

SCAVENGERS
Meat-eating dinosaurs may have scavenged their meat. Here, a group of *Ceratosaurus* feed from an *Allosaurus* kill.

LOOK OUT FOR THESE

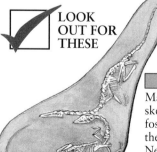

COELOPHYSIS
Masses of dinosaur skeletons which fossilized together, like these *Coelophysis* from New Mexico, show that some dinosaurs hunted in packs.

BARYONYX
This 30cm claw belonging to *Baryonyx* was probably used for hooking fish out of rivers.

MEGALOSAURUS
A *Megalosaurus* jaw with teeth was the first dinosaur fossil to be identified. It was found in Jurassic rock in England before 1820. The sharp teeth were used for tearing flesh.

UNUSUAL MEAT-EATERS

Some meat-eating dinosaurs were 12m long, like *Spinosaurus*. However, this dinosaur was probably quite lightly-built.

Oviraptor was a fast-running meat-eater with a strange bird-like head.

Oviraptor   *Spinosaurus*

FAST HUNTERS

Small meat-eaters could chase their prey, such as lizards and other small dinosaurs. They may also have stolen other hunters' meat, like these *Ornitholestes* have.

TYRANNOSAURUS

Tyrannosaurus was probably the biggest meat-eating dinosaur. It had a huge head and the great jaws held teeth up to 15cm long. These 'tyrant kings' walked upright on powerful legs. Their arms were tiny, however. .

NANOTYRANNUS

The skulls of meat-eating dinosaurs were very lightly built and were often destroyed before fossilization.

FOOTPRINTS

Meat-eating dinosaurs had three main toes. You can tell by the footprints they left.

BIGGEST DINOSAURS

The first dinosaurs were meat-eaters, but soon plant-eaters came along as well. Plant-eating animals need a much bigger gut than meat-eating ones, and so plant-eaters have longer bodies. They went about on four legs to support the greater weight, and developed long necks to reach their food.

These long-necked plant-eaters became the biggest land animals that ever lived. Their heyday was in the late Jurassic period.

HERDS
Masses of fossil footprints show that long-necked plant-eaters, like these *Omeisaurus*, may have lived in herds.

LATE FORMS OF PLANT-EATER
Some long-necked plant-eaters survived until the end of the Cretaceous period, especially in South America, where strange forms developed. *Saltasaurus* was unusual in having armour on its back. *Amargasaurus* had a sail-like crest on its neck.

LOOK OUT FOR THESE

GOING FOR LENGTH
Diplodocus was 27m long. Spines over the hips supported muscles which allowed it to rear up on its hind legs.

LONG SKULLS
Diplodocus and its relatives had long heads with narrow peg-like teeth.

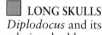

GOING FOR HEIGHT
Brachiosaurus was one of the tallest dinosaurs and had a neck that stretched up from high shoulders. It could reach up to 12m. It may have fed on the tops of trees, like a giraffe.

SMALL TYPES

Not all the plant-eaters were huge. *Shunosaurus* was only 10m long – a third of the length of the biggest.

LONG NECKS

Some plant-eaters, like *Mamenchisaurus* from China, had necks which, at more than 10m, were as long as the body and tail.

■ **BOX-LIKE SKULLS**

Brachiosarus and its relatives had short heads, with broad nostrils set high up on the skull.

■ **ULTRASAURUS**

There is no full skeleton of *Ultrasaurus*, but there are models of its leg bones. *Ultrasaurus* was even bigger than *Brachiosaurus*.

■ **FOOTPRINTS**

The long-necked plant-eaters left huge fossil footprints.

TWO-FOOTED PLANT-EATERS

Although most plant-eating dinosaurs walked about on all fours, there was a large group that could walk on two feet. These had a hip-bone with a gap beneath, so the big plant-digesting gut could be carried between the legs and the animal could still balance.

These upright dinosaurs, such as *Iguanodon,* evolved in the late Triassic period but they really came into their own in Cretaceous times. The later types had very strong grinding teeth and cheek pouches, so that they could eat tough conifer needles.

HEAVY TWO-FOOTED DINOSAURS

Big two-footed plant-eaters, like the 10m-long *Iguanodon,* lived in herds. They may have spent some of their time on all fours. They used their beak-like snout to tear off leaves.

THUMB SPIKE

The hand was shaped like a boxing glove with a spike for a thumb which they used in fights.

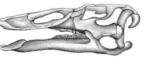

SPRINTERS

Lightweight plant-eaters, like the 2m-long *Hypsilophodon,* were built for speed and could run fast to escape danger.

LOOK OUT FOR THESE

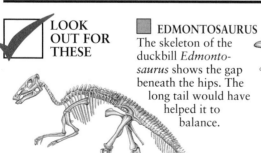

EDMONTOSAURUS
The skeleton of the duckbill *Edmontosaurus* shows the gap beneath the hips. The long tail would have helped it to balance.

ANATOSAURUS
This common duckbill had a very long flat head with a bill-like mouth. This unusual feature has given the group its name.

PARASAUROLOPHU
The longest crest of all was found on this duckbill. It was a hollow tube linked to the nose.

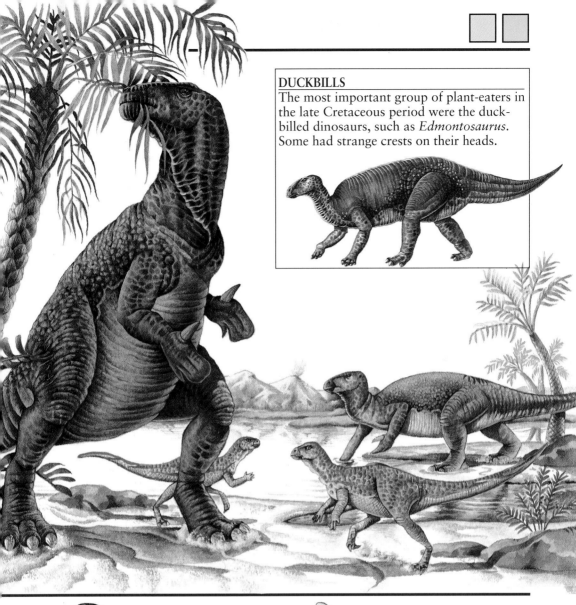

DUCKBILLS

The most important group of plant-eaters in the late Cretaceous period were the duck-billed dinosaurs, such as *Edmontosaurus*. Some had strange crests on their heads.

CORYTHOSAURUS
This was a large duckbill with a hollow crest like an ancient Greek helmet. The tubes in the crest could have helped it to make loud calls.

SAUROLOPHUS
Some duckbill crests were solid spikes. It is now thought that different sexes had different-sized crests.

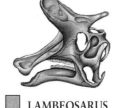

LAMBEOSARUS
This duckbill had a square crest with a spike sticking out at the back.

NESTS
Dinosaurs laid eggs in nests. This is known because fossil nesting sites belonging to the duckbill *Maiasaura* have been found.

PLATED AND ARMOURED DINOSAURS

The plated dinosaurs developed in the Jurassic period. These dinosaurs had a double row of plates and spines along their backs. They may have been used for armour, or they may have regulated the body's temperature. The dinosaur could have warmed its blood by turning the plates to the sun, or cooled it by holding up the plates in the wind.

The true armoured dinosaurs evolved in the late Cretaceous period. These had barrel-shaped bodies and their backs were covered with armour.

CLUBS AND SPIKES

Euoplocephalus was a typical armoured dinos that defended itself by swinging its large tail cl *Denversaurus* was another armoured dinosau but had spikes pointing sideways and forwards from its shoulders.

LOW PLATES

Wuherosaurus, from China, had plates that were long and low. But it did have some fierce spines along its tail.

THE SPINIEST

Kentrosaurus had long spines and very narrow plates. It had a pair of spines that stuck out over its hips.

LOOK OUT FOR THESE

SCELIDOSAURUS
This early Jurassic dinosaur was as big as a cow.

TEETH
The small teeth of *Scelidosaurus* were like those of a modern plant-eating lizard, for example, an iguana.

STEGOSAURUS
Several museums have mounted skeletons of *Stegosaurus*, but scientists are still unsure about how the plates were arranged.

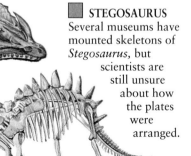

THE BIGGEST
Stegosaurus was 7.5m long and was the biggest of the plated dinosaurs. This dinosaur is also one of the best known.

SMALL PLATES
Another Chinese form, *Tuojiangosaurus,* had small conical plates all along its back.

■ STEGOSAURUS IN THE ROCK
Whenever a *Stegosaurus* skeleton fossil is found, the plates have all fallen over one another.

■ ARMOUR
The armour of an armoured dinosaur is usually so tough that it is easily fossilized, showing the bony plates and knobs.

■ SKULLS
The skulls of the club-tailed armoured dinosaurs had broad mouths. Those of the spiky armoured dinosaurs had narrow mouths.

HORNED DINOSAURS

Among the last dinosaurs to appear were the horned dinosaurs. These evolved from the two-footed plant-eaters at the end of the Cretaceous period. Unlike other dinosaurs, they had thick heavy skulls which were covered in armour, and had up to three horns pointing forwards. They used these horns to defend themselves and their herds against the great meat-eaters, like *Tyrannosaurus*. When their fossils where first found, in Colorado, USA, people thought they were from extinct giant bison.

THE BIGGEST

The biggest horned dinosaur was *Triceratops*, which was 9m long and weighed 5 tonnes. It roamed the forests in herds.

THE SMALLEST

Tiny *Leptoceratops* was only about the size of a turkey, but it lived at the same time as the giant *Triceratops*.

LOOK OUT FOR THESE

TRICERATOPS
Most horned dinosaur skeletons were very similar to this one of *Triceratops*. Only the size and the skulls differed.

CENTROSAURUS
Some horned dinosaurs had just a single horn on the nose as well as a bony frill.

PACHYRHINOSAURUS
This horned dinosaur has no horn! Or at least, it only had a small one up on the frill.

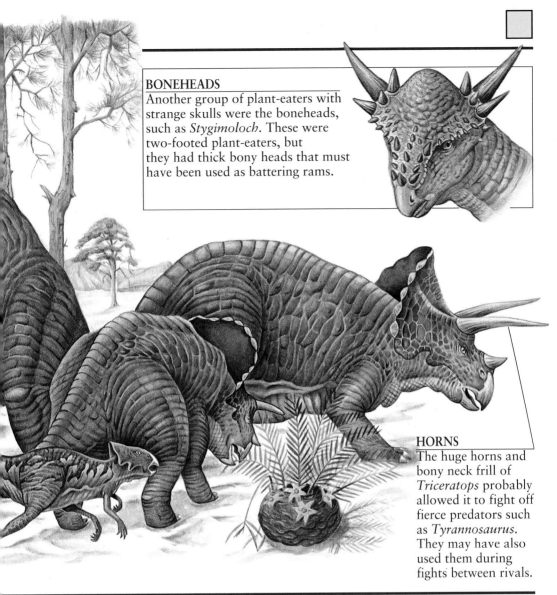

BONEHEADS
Another group of plant-eaters with strange skulls were the boneheads, such as *Stygimoloch*. These were two-footed plant-eaters, but they had thick bony heads that must have been used as battering rams.

HORNS
The huge horns and bony neck frill of *Triceratops* probably allowed it to fight off fierce predators such as *Tyrannosaurus*. They may have also used them during fights between rivals.

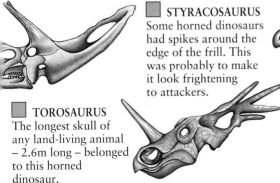

TOROSAURUS
The longest skull of any land-living animal – 2.6m long – belonged to this horned dinosaur.

STYRACOSAURUS
Some horned dinosaurs had spikes around the edge of the frill. This was probably to make it look frightening to attackers.

CHASMOSAURUS
This frill was very broad and lightweight. It was probably brightly-coloured and used for signalling.

STEGOCERAS
The skulls of the boneheads were very thick. *Stegoceras* means 'horny roof'.

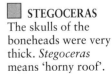

THE MAMMAL AGE DAWNS

What happens when most of the animal groups of the world become extinct at the same time? Nature tries again.

This happened after all the dinosaurs and all sorts of other creatures vanished at the end of the Cretaceous period. Why they suddenly died out is a mystery, but we know that immediately afterwards, the mammals took over. The mammals had evolved from the mammal-like reptiles but had remained as tiny, mouse-like animals throughout the age of the dinosaurs.

THE NEW COAL FORESTS
The forests of the early Tertiary period formed the brown coal deposits of Germany.

FLYING MAMMALS
Bats evolved to take the place of the pterosaurs.

ODDITIES
Some mammals were quite unlike any animals today. It is as if new designs were being tried out.

PLANT-EATERS
Pig-like mammals rooted through the undergrowth.

LOOK OUT FOR THESE

MESSELOBUNODON
The family of this long-legged mammal eventually evolved into the running mammals, such as antelopes.

LEPTICTIDIUM
This was an odd little jumping mammal which died out leaving no descendants.

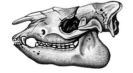

LOPHIODON
This was a plant-eating mammal like a modern tapir.

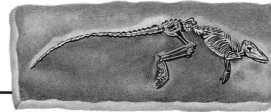

HUNTERS
Meat-eating mammals fed on the wide variety of plant-eaters.

ANTEATERS
Insects were common, and soon mammals evolved that fed on them.

HEDGEHOGS
Some animals had armour to protect themselves from meat-eaters.

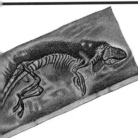

■ **EUROTAMANDUA**
This anteater was practically identical to the modern South American forms.

■ **MIACIS**
Miacis was a cat-like meat-eater.

■ **PHOLIDOCERCUS**
Pholidocercus was an early type of hedgehog.

■ **PALAEOCHIROPTERYX**
This was an early bat, it was very similar to modern bats.

GRASSLAND MAMMALS

About half-way through the Tertiary period, the landscape began to change. The forests that had sheltered all the strange mammals of earlier times began to die back and they were replaced by open grasslands.

As this happened, new mammals evolved that were more suited to living on the grassy plains. Creatures began to evolve that looked something like today's animals.

HOOVES
Running animals evolved. Their long legs and light hooves enabled them to run swiftly away from danger.

SWIFT HUNTERS
Fleet-footed meat-eaters evolved to hunt the fast-running grass-eaters.

THE BIGGEST MAMMAL
Probably the biggest land mammal ever was *Indricotherium*, a rhinoceros as big as a house.

LOOK OUT FOR THESE

DAPHONEUS
This early fleet-footed dog, rather like a long-tailed greyhound, had strong jaws with killing and meat-eating teeth.

MOROPUS
This was a distant relative of the horse, but it had claws instead of hooves. It must have fed on trees.

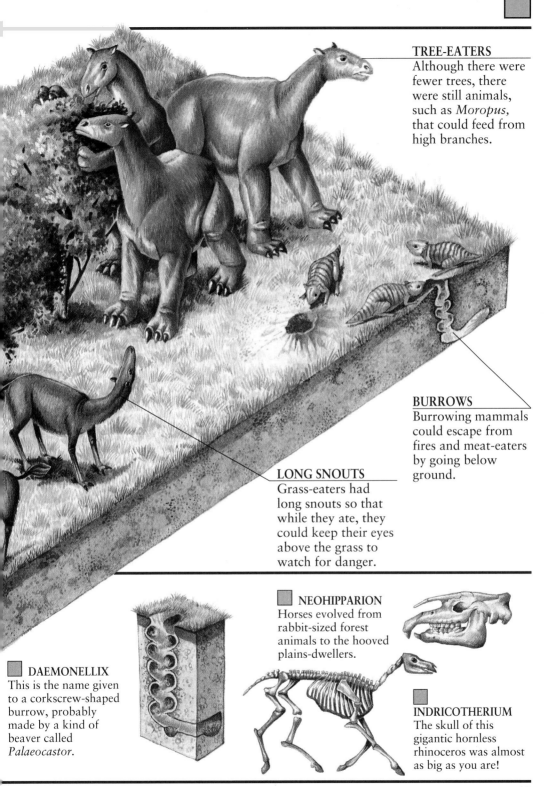

TREE-EATERS
Although there were fewer trees, there were still animals, such as *Moropus,* that could feed from high branches.

BURROWS
Burrowing mammals could escape from fires and meat-eaters by going below ground.

LONG SNOUTS
Grass-eaters had long snouts so that while they ate, they could keep their eyes above the grass to watch for danger.

NEOHIPPARION
Horses evolved from rabbit-sized forest animals to the hooved plains-dwellers.

DAEMONELLIX
This is the name given to a corkscrew-shaped burrow, probably made by a kind of beaver called *Palaeocastor.*

INDRICOTHERIUM
The skull of this gigantic hornless rhinoceros was almost as big as you are!

THE ICE AGE

The end of the Tertiary period saw a great cooling of climates throughout the world. The result was the Ice Age of the Quaternary period. During this time, the ice caps spread outwards from the South and North Poles, and the glaciers crept down from the mountains. The lowlands of northern Europe and North America had a chill tundra landscape – barren lands with frozen ground – like modern Siberia. Animals evolved that were adapted to a very cold climate. However, there were warm spells in the Ice Age, lasting tens of thousands of years.

SPECIAL DIET
The Irish elk could live on the sparse mosses and grasses of the bleak landscape. They roamed in herds like today's reindeer.

WOOLLY PELT
Many animals, such as the woolly rhinoceros, an extinct relative of the modern rhinos, had furry coats to keep them warm.

LOOK OUT FOR THESE

FROZEN MAMMOTH
Ice Age animals are often buried and preserved in frozen mud, such as this baby mammoth from Siberia.

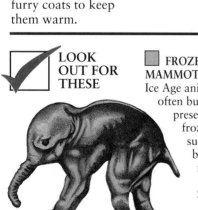

SABRE-TOOTHED TIGER
Mammoths and other big animals were prey to cats with enormous slashing teeth. The bones of these cats were found in tar pits.

EARLY ART
The drawings made on cave walls by people at the time give us an idea what Ice Age animals looked like.

LARGE SIZE

Big animals, like woolly mammoths, kept their heat in better than small animals, and so were suited to cold climates. Their long woolly fur also helped to protect them from the cold.

INTELLIGENCE

One creature survived the Ice Age by having the intelligence and ability to make clothing and shelters. This creature could make and use fire and tools. This, of course, was a human being.

RHINOCEROS
This rhinoceros was mummified in salt and asphalt in a pit in Poland.

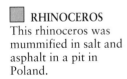

WOOLLY RHINOCEROS
The skull of a rhinoceros does not show the horn. This is because it is made of tightly-packed hair.

IRISH ELK ANTLERS
Thousands of antlers with spans of up to 2.5m have been found in peat bogs in Ireland.

TOOLS AND WEAPONS
The animals of the Ice Age were hunted by tribes of humans with tools made of wood, bone and stone.

GLOSSARY

Words in SMALL CAPITAL letters indicate a cross-reference.

ammonite One of an extinct group of animals, related to the octopus and squid, that lived in a coiled shell that is often found fossilized. One of the commonest fossils.

amphibian A member of the group of animals, like the frogs and newts, that usually lay eggs in the water, live as a swimming tadpole when young, but spend most of their lives on land when adult.

antennae Organs that stick out from the head of an INVERTEBRATE and allow the animal to sense things around it. Often called feelers.

arthropod An INVERTEBRATE animal with jointed body and jointed legs. Insects, spiders and crabs are arthropods.

bed A single layer of SEDIMENTARY ROCK.

belemnite An extinct animal related to the squids, with a bullet-shaped shell that is often found as a FOSSIL.

brachiopod A sea animal encased in two shells, unrelated to the modern bivalve molluscs, that was much more common in times past, and whose shells are commonly found as FOSSILS.

cephalon The head shield of a TRILOBITE.

conifer A tree that reproduces by means of cones. Pines and fir trees are modern conifers.

continental shelf The edge of the continent that is covered by the sea. This produces shallow waters around the dry land.

convergent evolution The rule of EVOLUTION that states that similar body shapes evolve in different animals in response to the same environmental conditions. Dolphins, sharks and ICHTHYOSAURS all have the same streamlined shape but are unrelated.

coral An INVERTEBRATE animal that grows in one place like a plant and secretes a hard shell around itself. Many corals living together can form a REEF.

dinosaur One of a group of reptiles that were very important during the Triassic, Jurassic and Cretaceous PERIODS.

evolution The process of change over a number of generations which produces new species.

fossil A part or a trace of a once-living organism preserved in rocks.

gill An organ that allows a water-living animal to extract oxygen from the water.

hoof A toe nail that has evolved for walking on, as in a horse.

ice age A time in the history of the Earth when climates were particularly cold.

ichthyosaur One of a group of extinct marine reptiles, that looked rather like dolphins through CONVERGENT EVOLUTION.

invertebrate An animal without a backbone or internal skeleton.

limestone A SEDIMENTARY ROCK consisting largely of the mineral calcite.

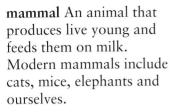

mammal An animal that produces live young and feeds them on milk. Modern mammals include cats, mice, elephants and ourselves.

mammal-like reptiles One of a group of early REPTILES that had certain mammal characteristics – hair, teeth, leg shape – and later evolved into the MAMMALS themselves.

marine Living in the sea.

mosasaur A type of extinct MARINE reptile, related to the modern lizards.

nodule A lump of mineral that has grown round something embedded in the rock.

period In geological terms a particular span of Earth history which is characterized by the animals and plants that lived. Rocks formed in that period can be identified by the FOSSILS of these animals and plants.

plesiosaur A type of extinct swimming REPTILE.

pterosaur A type of extinct flying REPTILE.

reconstruction Fossil bones that have been reassembled and mounted, usually in a museum display, to show how the complete skeleton would have looked.

reef An underwater rocky outcrop that comes close to the surface. Usually a reef is built up over many years from the shells of CORALS, sponges or other sea creatures.

reptile A VERTEBRATE cold-blooded animal that reproduces by laying a hard-shelled or leathery egg. Lizards, snakes and crocodiles are modern reptiles.

restoration A model, drawing or painting of the prehistoric animal to show how it might have appeared in life.

scavenger An animal that feeds by eating the dead bodies of others.

sediment Loose material such as sand or mud that accumulates on the floor of a sea or a river.

sedimentary rock A rock made from solidified SEDIMENT.

suture line The line along which one part of a shell joins another.

tentacle A limb that has no internal skeleton.

thecodont A type of REPTILE from which the DINOSAURS evolved.

thorax The middle section of an ARTHROPOD's body.

trace fossil A FOSSIL that contains no part of the original organism but shows where the organism lived, such as a burrow or a footprint.

trilobite A member of a group of extinct ARTHROPODS that lived in the sea in Palaeozoic times.

tundra Cold lands characterized by permafrost – frozen soil in which only the top layers thaw out during the summer. This produces landscapes of bogs and lakes, where few trees grow.

vertebrate An animal that has an internal skeleton based on a backbone. Fish, AMPHIBIANS, REPTILES, birds and MAMMALS are vertebrates.

INDEX